FLAVAZS LIQUORS

ELISA HAMILTON

AuthorHouse™
1663 Liberty Drive
Bloomington, IN 47403
www.authorhouse.com
Phone: 833-262-8899

This book is printed on acid-free paper.

ISBN: 979-8-8230-0828-0 (sc)
ISBN: 979-8-8230-0829-7 (e)

Library of Congress Control Number: 2023908956

Print information available on the last page.

Published by AuthorHouse 05/10/2023

authorHOUSE®

TABLE OF CONTENTS

CRANBERRY COCKTAIL

INGREDIENTS
2/3 cup Cranberry juice
1/4 cup Patron Silver tequila
1 oz. Triple Sec
1/2 Lime (Juiced)
Ice
Desired or favorite garnish

INSTRUCTIONS
- Add cranberry juice, tequila, triple sec, lime & Ice in a Cocktail Shaker & shake all ingredients until chilled.
- Pour contents in a glass
- Add desired garnish
- Drink & enjoy!

PLUM MARTINI

INGREDIENTS

5 plums (chopped with skin & seed removed)

2 oz. lime juice

1 oz. simple syrup

2 oz. white rum

Ice

Desired garnish

INSTRUCTIONS

- Combine all ingredients in a Cocktail Shaker & shake well.
- Pour in a glass
- Add your desired garnish
- Drink & enjoy!

ORANGE CARROT COCKTAIL

INGREDIENTS
1/4 cup vodka
1/2 cup orange juice (chilled)
1/2 cup carrot juice (chilled)
2 1/2 tsp. lime juice (chilled)
Garnish as desired

INSTRUCTIONS
- Add all ingredients in a Cocktail
  Shaker & shake well.
- Pour in a glass
- Garnish as desired
- Drink & enjoy!

CITRUS COCKTAIL

INGREDIENTS

2 oz. Cointreau citrus triple sec

Garnish with 1/2 of a slice of orange

3 oz. prosecco

2 oz. Aperol

1 oz. club soda

Ice

INSTRUCTIONS

- Add all ingredients in a Cocktail Shaker & shake well.
- Pour in a glass
- Garnish with an orange slice.
- Serve & enjoy!

MANGO CARROT COCKTAIL

INGREDIENTS
5 oz. Malibu Mango Rum

4 cups of Carrot Juice

6 oz. Roca Patron Reposado

2 cups of Goya Mango Vodka

5 oz. Barcardi Mango Rum

Ice

INSTRUCTIONS
- Combine all the above ingredients in a blender and mix smoothly
- Pour the blended drink in a glass and add Ice.
- Drink and enjoy!

X-RATED PASSION

INGREDIENTS
1 3/4 cups of passion fruit puree
Ice
3 tbsps. of honey
2 oz. Wray & Nephew wite rum
1/2 cup water
2 oz. Smirnoff Passionfruit fruit Vodka

INSTRUCTIONS
* Combine all ingredients in a blender and mix smoothly.
* Pour mixed contents from the blender into a glass.
* Garnish if desired
* Drink and enjoy!

CARROT PUNCH

INGREDIENTS

10 carrots (chopped)

2 cans of Grace condensed milk

1 can of Grace Evaporated milk

2 -3 tsps. vanilla extract

2 tsps. ground cinnamon

2 tsps. ground cinnamon

2 tsps. nutmeg

iNSTRUCTIONS

- Add all ingredients to a blender and mix smoothly.
- Pour blended mixture in a pitcher and put in the fridge to cool.
- Remove from the fridge and pour in a glass and add Ice.
- Serve and enjoy!

BLACKBERRY BLAZE

INGREDIENTS
2.5 oz. blackberry schnapps

1 3/4 cups blackberry puree

2.5 oz. Ciroc Vodka

Ice

3 tbsps. honey

iNSTRUCTIONS
- Combine all ingredients in a blender and mix smoothly.
- Pour mixed contents from blender into a glass and add Ice.
- Garnish if desired.
- Drink and enjoy!

NOCTURNAL NECTAR

INGREDIENTS
1 3/4 cups of Nectar puree
1/4 cup pineapple
3 tbsps. honey
2.5 oz. Absolut Vodka
3 oz. Absolut Peach Vodka
Ice

INSTRUCTIONS
- Combine all ingredients in a blender and mix smoothly.
- Pour mixed contents from blender into a glass and add Ice.
- Garnish if desired.
- Drink and enjoy!

HAWAIIAN HOLIDAY

INGREDIENTS

2 cups of Minute Maid

4 oz. of Van Gogh mango vodka

4 oz. of Bacardi Superior Rum

3 tsps. of fresh lemon juice

2 oz. of Smirnoff Peach Vodka

Ice

INSTRUCTIONS

- Combine all ingredients in a blender and mix smoothly.
- Pour mixed contents in a glass.
- Serve and enjoy!

SEXUAL SEDUCTION

INGREDIENTS

1 can of Coconut milk

1 can of Condensed milk

1/2 cup of Evaporated milk

9.6 oz. pack of Grace Irish Moss

2 tsps. Vanilla extract

2 tsps. ground cinnamon

2 tsps. nutmeg

INSTRUCTIONS

- Put Irish moss in a container with 1 lemon cut into 2 pieces; cover and let sit overnight.
- Wash several times with cool water, remove any debris and drain water from the container.
- Put Irish moss on stove with cinnamon water.
- Add all the rest of the above ingredients in a blender and mix smoothly.
- Add Ice, serve and enjoy!

TROPICAL ERUPTION

INGREDIENTS
1 3/4 cup Mango puree
1 3/4 cup Pineapple puree
3 oz. Mango tequila
2 tsps. lemon juice
2.5 oz. peach triple sec.
2 oz. Wray & Nephew white rum
3 tsps. honey
Orange slice & mint for garnish
Ice

INSTRUCTIONS
- Add all ingredients to a blender and mix well.
- Pour in a glass and add garnish
- Drink and enjoy!

PEANUT PUNCH

INGREDIENTS

1 cup of raw peanuts

1 can of condensed milk

2 tsps. vanilla essence

1 tsp. cinnamon powder

Ice

1 tsp. nutmeg (grated)

1/2 cup of water

1/2 cup of water

1/2 cup of Supligen

1/2 cup of evaporated milk

INSTRUCTIONS

- Blend all ingredients in a blender and mix smoothly.
- Pour blended mixture in a glass.
- Serve and enjoy!

ENTANGLEMENT

INGREDIENTS

1/2 cup to 1 cup of Lucozade

3 tbsps. honey

1/3 cup of water

Ice

1 3/4 cup Guava puree

1 3/4 cup of Passionfruit puree

2.5 oz. Malibu pineapple white rum

4 oz. tequila

2 oz. orange triple sec

INSTRUCTIONS

- Combine all ingredients in a Cocktail Shaker and mix well.
- Pour contents in a glass.
- Serve and enjoy!

CHAMPION STALLION

INGREDIENTS
1 tsp. nutmeg

1 tbsp. vanilla extract

1 tsp. cinnamon powder

1/2 cup of coconut milk

2 green plantains (chopped and boiled in water)

1 can of condensed milk

1/2 cup of dragon stout

INSTRUCTIONS
- Boil plantains in a pot on medium-high heat until cooked.
- Remove plantains from the stove and add to the blender along with all the above mentioned ingredients and allow mixture to blend smoothly.
- Let cool in the fridge; Serve with Ice and enjoy!

PLANTAIN PUNCH

INGREDIENTS

1/2 cup of Guiness

3 plantains (boiled and chopped)

2 tsp. Vanilla essence

1/2 cup of oats

1 cup of Supligen

1 can of condensed milk

1 tsp. ground cinnamon

1 tsp. ground nutmeg

INSTRUCTIONS

- Boil plantains in a pot on medium-high heat until cooked.
- Remove plantains from the stove and add to the blender along with all the above mentioned ingredients and allow contents to blend smoothly.
- Let cool in the fridge; Serve with Ice and enjoy!

STRAWBERRY WATERMELON COCKTAIL

INGREDIENTS

2 cups of Strawberries

2 cups of Watermelon

Ice

3 cups of V8 Splash fruit medley Juice

6 oz. Smirnoff Strawberry Rose Vodka

3 tbsps. maple syrup

INSTRUCTIONS

- Put all above ingredients in a blender and mix smoothly

INSTRUCTIONS

- Put all the above ingredients in a blender and mix smoothly.
- Serve and enjoy!

OKRA PUNCH

INGREDIENTS

12 Okras (Cooked)

1 Guiness

3 tsps. Vanilla essence

2 tsps. nutmeg

1 tsp. ground cinnamon powder

1 can of condensed milk

1 cup of whole milk or milk of choice

1/2 cup of Oats

INSTRUCTIONS

- Boil okra in 1 cup of water for about 8-10 minutes.
- Put the rest of the above mentioned ingredients in a blender and mix smoothly.
- Pour mixed contents in a pitcher and let cool in the fridge.
- Remove cooled contents from the fridge.
- Serve and enjoy!

MANGO WATERMELON COCKTAIL

INGREDIENTS
1 Mango (Skin removed and chopped)
1/2 of Mango puree
2 cups of watermelon (chopped)
4 oz. Absolut Mango Vodka
4 oz. Ciroc Watermelon Vodka
Ice

INSTRUCTIONS
- Put all ingredients in a blender and mix smoothly.
- Pour contents in a pitcher and put in the fridge to cool.
- Remove the pitcher from the fridge.
- Pour Cocktail beverage in a glass.
- Drink and enjoy!

MANGO KIWI COCKTAIL

INGREDIENTS

5 kiwis (peeled and chopped)
1 pack (14 oz.) Goya Mango pulp
Ice
3 tbsps. of simple syrup
5 oz. Smirnoff Mango Vodka
5 oz. Kiwi Cuvee
3 oz. Sauvignon
Blanc White Wine

INSTRUCTIONS

- Add kiwi to a Blender and blend until smooth.
- Strain the blended kiwi with a strainer and omit the seeds from the juiced fruit.
- Put the strained kiwi juice in the blender; add the rest of the above mentioned ingredients and blend till smooth.
- Pour mixed contents in a pitcher and let cool in the fridge
- Remove from the fridge, pour in a glass and Serve and enjoy!

BANANA BLUEBERRY COCKTAIL

INGREDIENTS
4 bananas (peeled and chopped)
1 cup of blueberries
5 oz. Bacardi Banana Rum
4 oz. Roberto Cavalli vodka
Ice

INSTRUCTIONS
• Put all ingredients in a blender and mix smoothly.
• Pour blended drink in a pitcher and put in the fridge to cool.
• Remove from the fridge.
• Drink and enjoy!

THUNDERBOLT

INGREDIENTS
2 oz. Brandy
2 cups of Apricot Juice
2.5 oz. Gin
4 oz. Grenadine
1 oz. Lemon Juice
Ice

INSTRUCTIONS
- Put all ingredients in a Cocktail Shaker and mix well.
- Pour in a glass
- Drink and enjoy!

GLADIATOR

INGREDIENTS

1 cup of Oats

1 cup of cashews

1 can of condensed milk

1 cup of Supligen (Vanilla flavor:cold)

3 tsps. Vanilla extract

2 tsps. nutmeg

3 tbsps. of Peanut butter

Ice

INSTRUCTIONS

- Add all the above mentioned ingredients to a blender and ensure that all ingredients are blended smoothly.
- Pour mixed content from the blender in a glass.
- Drink and enjoy!

TSUNAMI COCKTAIL DRINK

INGREDIENTS

1 cup of Lucozade (Original Flavor: Cold)
1 pack of a 14 oz. Goya Guava pulp
3 tbsps. honey
5 oz. DeKuyper Red Apple Schnapps
4.5 oz. Seagrams Watermelon Vodka
1 cup of Apple Juice (cold)
Ice

INSTRUCTIONS

- Add all ingredients to a blender and mix smoothly.
- Pour contents in a glass
- Serve, drink and enjoy!

BEDROOM BANDIT

INGREDIENTS

1 cup of Oats

3 tsps. Vanilla extract

2 1/2 tsps. nutmeg

1 can of condensed milk

1 pack of 14 oz. Goya Soursop pulp

1 cup of Almonds

2 tsps. cinnamon

1 cup of cashew

1 cup of Nutrament (cold)

Ice

INSTRUCTIONS

- Put all the above listed ingredients in a blender and ensure all contents are mixed smoothly.
- Pour mixture in a glass
- Serve and enjoy!

MANGO BLUEBERRY COCKTAIL

INGREDIENTS
1 1/2 cups of blueberries
2 cups of Mango (peeled and chopped)
4 oz. Amoretti Mango Craft Puree
4 oz. Barefoot Fruitscato Blueberry White
wine
4 oz. Dekuyper Blueberry Schnapps
Ice

INSTRUCTIONS
• Put all the above listed ingredients in a
blender and mix smoothly.
• Pour mixed drink in a pitcher and let
cool in the fridge.
• Remove the pitcher from the fridge
and pour contents in a glass.
• Drink and enjoy!

ABOUT THE AUTHOR

Elisa Hamilton is an Author, Content Creator, and a Food & Drink Connoisseur. Her writing style can best be described as creative, passionate, and intriguing. Writing has been a significant part of her life, and she has been creating stories & poems since she was young. In her free time, she enjoys reading books, creating & writing books, cooking, drink making, learning, and exploring new cultures, arts & entertainment. She looks forward to sharing more of her writing with you in the future from her diverse genre of books.

Thank you for taking the time to read her Author bio and she hopes you enjoy making and drinking the delightful liquors in Flavazs Liquors Drink Book.

Printed in the United States
by Baker & Taylor Publisher Services